Praise

"Alycia's poems are urgent, important and satiating. Her work takes on patriarchy, ceremony, grief, motherhood and feasting in ways that are raw and expansive. The images that she weaves with her words speak of the lands she comes from and drip with texture that you can almost taste. This collection is critical and an ode to Two Spirit resurgence and all the complexities present of carrying generations of resilience in your bones and bodies."

- Seán Carson Kinsella
nêhi(y/th)aw/otipemisiwak/Nakawé/Irish poet and storyteller

"At turns fierce and tender, The Feast explores the dichotomies of the human condition, bringing us from rage to joy, scarcity to abundance, violence to peace. Ultimately, this is a love letter. To the poet's culture, her sexuality, her children, her family, and perhaps most radically… her self."

- Ashley J.J. White, Writers' Guild of Alberta

"Alycia Two Bears' work is poignant, stark, and entirely beautiful. Her voice dances between the soft playfulness of love and sexuality and the reassurance of healing; her lines undulate on the page itself. All this sacredness is held together by dividing the book into the rounds of a sweat, where the heat becomes more intense, as does the healing. Alycia has put her whole being between the covers of this book. After the last line rolls through you, she'll be your lover, enraptured and frustrated with you. She will be your best friend and confidant, sipping tea, smiling her warm smile. She will be your Doula, your spiritual guide, a reassuring hug, and a comforting voice in the darkest hours. This work is much needed, and Alycia Two Bears has delivered it."

- Daniel Poitras, member of Paul's First Nation & poet

"Alycia Two Bears' poems delve into themes of motherhood, pain, healing, identity and passion with skill and confidence. Alycia's writing is provocative and rhapsodic – a celebration of words that's both carnal and clever. The Feast is soul-satiating."

- Kim Mannix, Writer & Author of *Confirm Humanity*

"The Feast is a tender loop through generations and geographies that embraces a fierce certainty. Lush and grounded, this sensual collection models an openness adept at holding the dynamic expanse of being."

- Samantha Jones – Author of *Attic Rain*

The Feast

Two Spirit: Stories, Sex and the Ceremony behind it all, and other Poems

Alycia Two Bears

© Alycia Two Bears

All rights reserved. No part of this publication may be reproduced, distributed, or transmitted in any form or by any means, including photocopying, recording, digital scanning, or other electronic or mechanical methods, without the prior written permission of the publisher, except in the case of brief quotations embodied in critical reviews and certain other non-commercial uses permitted by copyright law. For permission, please address Wild Skies Press.

Published 2025
Printed in Canada

ISBN Print 978-1-0693754-0-7

Cover Design by Alexis Marie Chute
Interior Artwork by AI
Interior Design by Alexis Marie Chute

For information address:
Wild Skies Press
A division of Alexis Marie Productions Inc.
Edmonton, Alberta, Canada
info@alexismariechute.com
www.WildSkiesPress.com

Wild Skies Press is an independent literary publisher founded in 2021. Wild Skies refers to the Aurora Borealis—northern lights—in Alberta, where the press is located, situated on Treaty 6 Territory. Wild Skies Press publishes non-fiction, fiction, poetry, and hybrid genres with an emphasis on the creation of Canadian works and books by emerging and established authors.
www.WildSkiesPress.com

I dedicate this version to everyone who has been told they weren't enough, while simultaneously, too much.

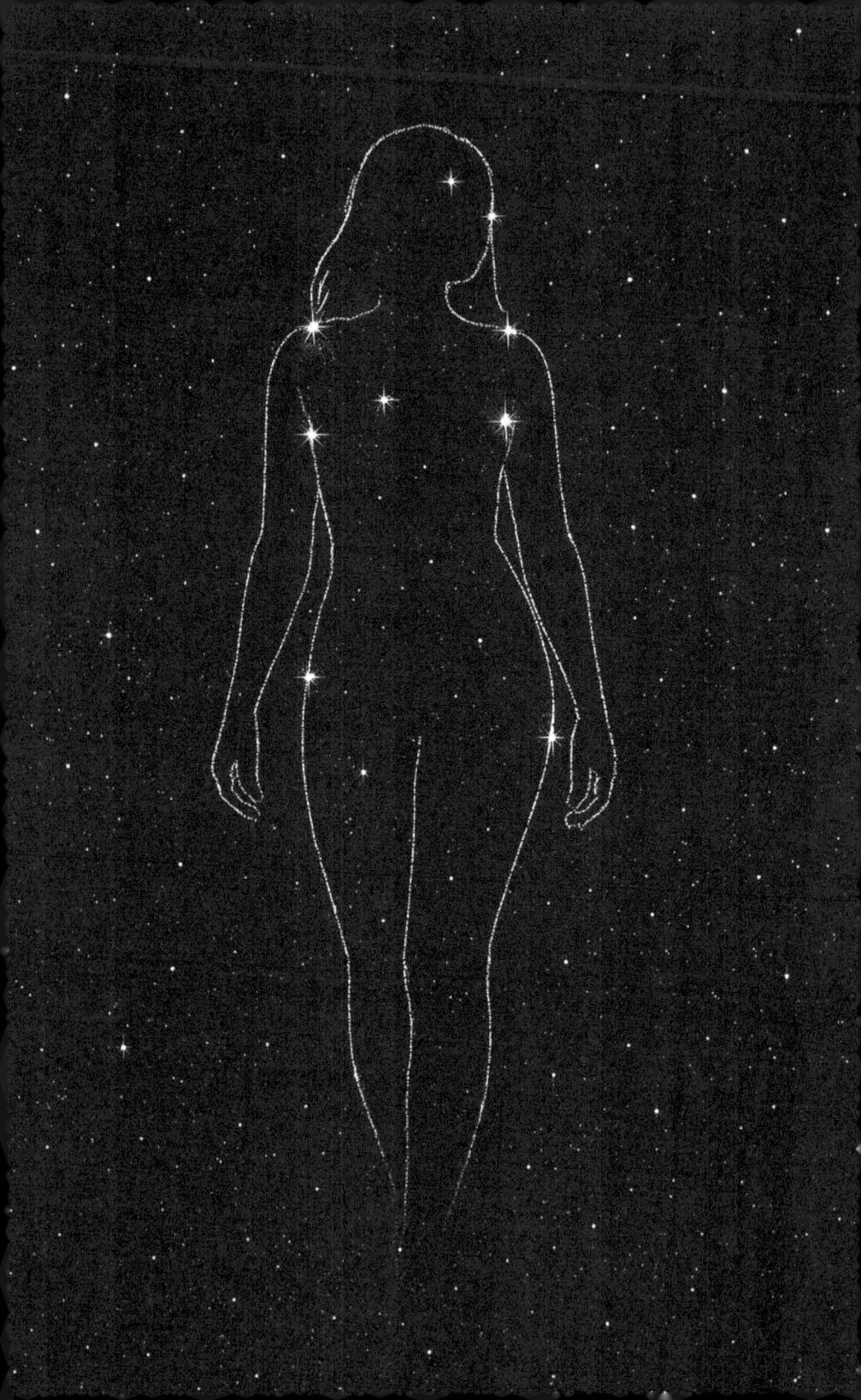

The Feast

Mint Tea
Two Spirit Odes and Identity
9

Berry Soup
Stories of Motherhood. My Children. Myself and the many forms love can come in
33

Smoked Salmon
Relationships: Fantasy, Dating, Sex and Break Ups
69

Sweet Treats
The Ceremony that holds me through it all
175

Mint Tea

Two Spirit Odes and Identity

Our Existence is Political

the shape of my brown eyes
the way my hair
holds in the heat of
the sun
my cheekbones
sloped and cut
like the mountains
I seek solace in
daily reminders
I come from this Land
my birth
a direct
refusal
of an on going
genocide
my whole existence is
political

Tired

I'm fucking tired
Not in a
Get some sleep
And enjoy a tea
Way
In a-
Can we fucking
Burn down the
Patriarchy
Churches based
In hate
That have already
Burnt women
Children
Men
For merely being
Born
As they are
.tired.

Bisexual

unless you are
invited to my
bed
it is none of
your business

Myself

and who do you write for?

myself

to give love and affection
in the ways in which
I desire to be consumed
I will write myself
into a dizzy
I will warm my own skin
I will make myself drunk
on my words and lust after my own thoughts

Texture Upon Texture

Elysian

Words all have their own texture to me.

Soft, smooth, run off the tongue.

Abrupt, rude, hard to swallow.

People are much like words to me.

Some are peanut butter vibes.

Some are good. Fine. Forgettable.

Soul stokers. Euphoric. Ecstasy.

Everybody has their own tone.

Texture.

Frequency.

Touch.

Mama Two Shoes had No Shoes

We met on the side of a mountain. It wasn't rocky, full of jagged edges or slippery shale fragments. It was green, soft moss everywhere, with scattered pieces of grey stone. The mountain side itself was steep, and I was afraid of rolling off the edge into oblivion. But not you. You tipsy-toed around the moss and open spaces. Light. Delicate. You moved with the strength and grace of a dancer. Sitting, holding tobacco and ribbon in my hand, I watched your flannel cherry red dress, with small yellow and white flower print, flap in the wind. I looked down in my lap. I was wearing my plain sunshine yellow sweat dress, it too was moving rapidly with the wind. I attempted to look back up at you, but my hair was furiously whipping around in the wind. I couldn't keep my eyes on you, to watch, observe and learn from you. Your hair was long again. Really long. Past your waist. Before cancer. It was thick, shiny and white. Oh, how I have missed that hair. I felt my heart ache. And that's when I saw it, our hair intertwined, dancing together in the winds. A mix of brown and white. This wind was strong, yes, but not cold. Not even chilly. It was only air swirling around us. As I turned my attention across the scene, I heard them first. Then I saw them running. Laughing. Full of joy. Free. My children. My blessings. You would think they were born of the mountain we perched on. No fear of falling, I called out to them to be careful around the edge. My voice caught in the wind and carried away from their sweet ears. She turned and smiled at me. With the slight turn of head again, she smiled at them, looked back at me and mouthed, "They're gonna be alright mama, let them be." I believed you. I always have. I stood up at your encouragement. Through the fear of being blown off the mountainside, I rose, clutching the tobacco into my palm. Standing, tall, proud, I raised the tobacco offering. I wondered, why this mountain. Why this place? This day? I follow her gaze. It was fixed on a Valley down below. Small, green, beautiful in its lush scenery. I heard another voice, from just beside me, another woman, unknown, she said, "That's her home y'know. That Valley. She just needed to see it. This is the only place she can see it from." We let our tobacco go, letting it spread to wherever it needed to be received. Letting our prayers spill all over the mountain.

Barb

steam rolls off the top
of our dark brown hair
retreating to the small trees
for reprieve
we snack on smoked salmon
berries
something I found at the
local all organic store
they are one of my greatest love stories
it is years full of
tears
laughter
babies
grief
ceremony
dancing
talking
being

Kay

deadleh nehiyaw accent
full of compassion
forgiveness
humour
love

enough for a whole community
to heal

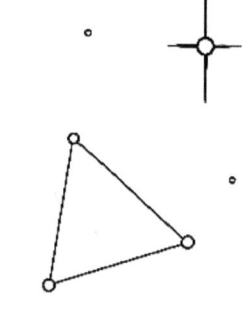

Beric

Vikings
Come in all forms
Not just by the sea
Whipping blonde hair and steel blue eyes
Sometimes they come to you in the night
Under the instructions of the moon
Asking you to come dance and release
They share witty antics and beautiful songs at 2am
They hold your hand and head high
They come in a long lean build
Sleek and smooth like a jaguar
Beautiful soft brown hair, warm caramel eyes
Utterly delectable, luscious lips
A soul so rare. Raw. Healing. Fucking brilliant.
(S)He came to me when I needed them most
A prayer answered. Ancestors knew it was time.
My Viking came in the quiet night and stayed.
I now and for always have a safe place to keep my soul.
heart.love.
Protector. Soul sister. Medicine.

Birth Day Ode To My Beautiful Beric

Vikings
You are the shift
Space in between
Snow melting
Seeds bursting
Green stalks reaching for the sun
A beautiful, delicate tapestry of life
Stretching out and across the lands
You are the space in between rest
And
Blossom
Celebrated every year
Equinox
Your warmth
Your grace
Your love is
The fluidity in the ways in which you move
In and out of
This
    Spirit….
        Art….
            Realm

So generous
Medicine in abundance

S/He

Was born
On spring equinox
This doesn't surprise me
The languid dancer
Between worlds
The bringer of Spring's sunlight
While embracing
Winter's long cold darkness
The giver of love
Joy
Art
Meaning
My beautiful Beric
Birthed
On the most perfect date
Look at all of us
Two legged ones
Four legged ones
Feathered ones
Mother Earth
Celebrating you
Every Year

J

Was never good with words
He mostly enjoyed
Chasing
Devouring
Me
In the woods
The backseat
The stairway
Wherever he could
Cause I tasted like nothing
He ever had in his 32 years
But once
He said, when he was not mine
When you came out of that Lodge
Your skin flushed from the steam
Your hair like a crown
Set up against the sun
Your yellow dress
Clinging to your curves
I fell in love with you, again
And remembered why
Men started wars
over women
Who look like you

Nadera

the type of woman
who uses lap dances as a warm up
a dirty grind to create heat
then when she asks you to tie her up
you understand what she meant
by being bound to the one
she desires
a love like Nadera
big ass
big heart
big fantasy
is for the man who wants it all
no time for playing small
she ain't got time for that shit

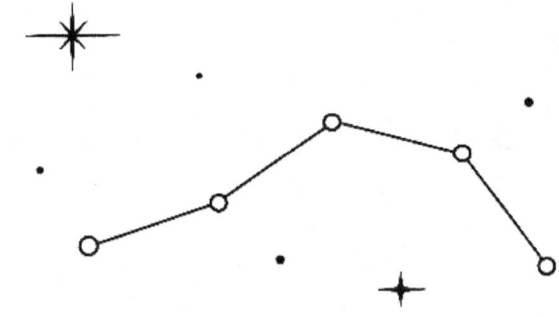

Johnny Noir

He loves
Angels, Goddesses & Revolution

I am a bit of all three

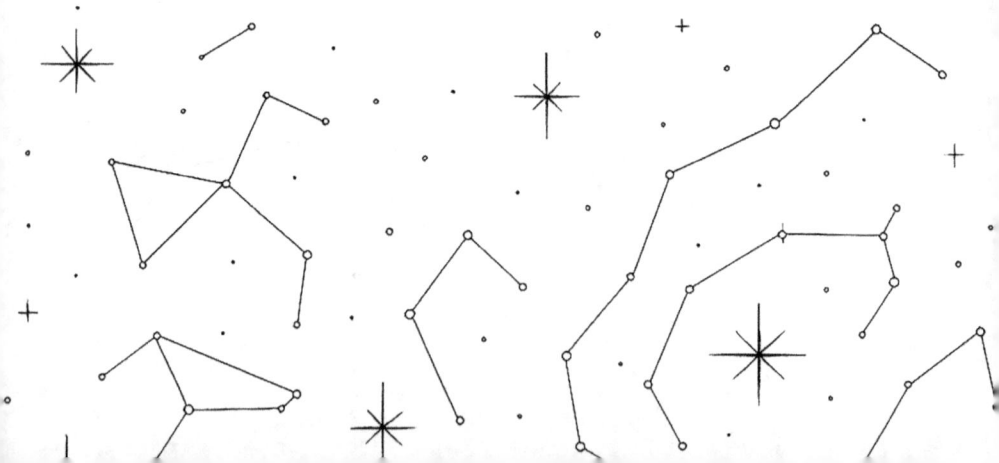

She Let Us Make Stars

It's been near a year.

What does that look like to you? That time.

Was it a walk in the meadow?

Sunlight streaming on your peach sun kissed face?

Arms sprawled out, fingertips grazing overgrown wheat in a Wildflower patch. A confused scenery. The way it was meant to be.

Did it feel like a heartbeat? The first strike on a drum?

A miniscule pause in time.

Half a breath.

With your smile, full, just as it was—still is, was how you looked in this dream.

Carefree. Beautiful.

The year here for us was not as easy.

But I do not want you to worry.

Listen to our prayers. Guide us. Love us.

Just as you always have.

Now when we say, the ancestors hear you.

It's you.

You are the ancestors.

So, please keep enjoying the endless blue sky.

Your joy is our answered prayers.

Self Identity

You can shave my
Head and I will still keep the prayers
Within the braids that fall
You can drain the blood from my body
The songs I know
Reside in my marrow
As languages fumble off my lips
Take away the earrings, slogan shirts
And ribbon skirts
And
I still know who I am
And
Whose lodge raised me

Two Bears

not dark
not gay
not queer
not loud
enough

:

Too dark
Too gay
Too queer
Too loud
Too much

Internalized Misogyny

weird
it smells
so much skin
it tastes nasty
it's gross
a joke

the introduction to the greatest portal between
the stars and earth

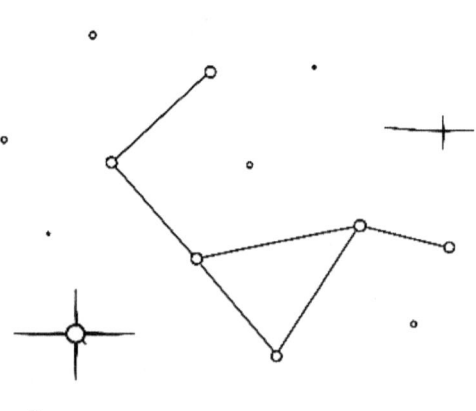

Of All the Names

The girl
  The woman
    The muse
     The mother
    The sage
     The longing
    The wanderer
   The writer
  The poet
  The grace
 The mercy
  The home
    The light
     The path
       The moon woman

An Ode to Myself

there are always going to be the basics
the love of burgundy lips, dresses, and wine
lace and leather
to bind and tear
the way I want to be bonded
to my lover
while cherishing the loud, boisterous
laughter of my children
who know their mother to the depths of her marrow
long legs, wild hair, limbs everywhere
heart radiating that white aura
with every beat
love shown on my sleeve
tattooed for permanence
dry, witty humour
deliciously dark and divine
I bring the light

Belong

toes dip
into
the Milky Way
slipping
into
somewhere
I feel I
belong

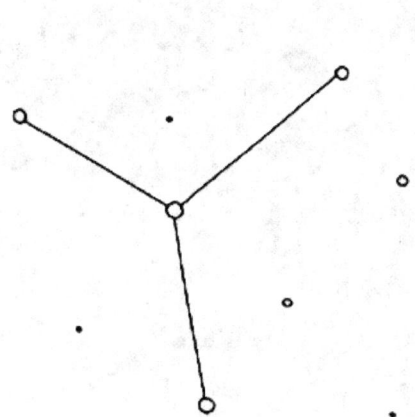

Berry Soup

Stories of Motherhood, My Children, Myself and the many forms love can come in

My Life

my life
is
curated
to the
ways
I want
mountains
tea
community
blind folded yoga
my children
my time and energy
are precious gifts
I only give
to whom I choose

My Maternal Blood Lines

I come from women who
hopped on trains and moved
two provinces away….

rejected middle class life
catching the next bus out of town

so no, I don't worry about
creating paths
       living fully
I fear boredom living in the mundane
    knowing I want so much more

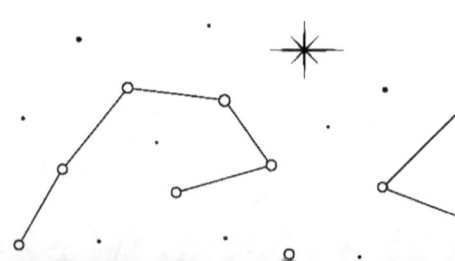

Should

suffocates

the way I should
mother
leaves me
deciding
drive/crash/drive/crash
should
lands me hospitals
should
stifling
with its rigid ways
born 4 weeks and 4 days
late
I never was one
who does what she should
I do what I want
when I so please

Single Parenthood

the feelings overwhelm
same as the lapping
of the Ocean
starting at your toes
only to find yourself
submerged
thrashing
pleading
for reprieve

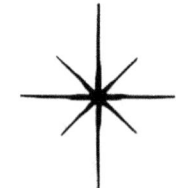

Euphoric

My life

Sunlight streams in

This gentle breathing

Slight snores

Of up to five not so little bodies

In my queen-sized bed

And one fat cat

Sweetgrass and incense

Fill the air

Morning yoga

Slowly waking

The babes from their slumber

My life

is

Euphoric

Mother of Storms

I wonder
if this is the
adventure
they were certain
they wanted when
they chose me
as their mother.
Driving towards
the dark clouds
tornado warning radio
full moon behind us
me telling them
you're safe go back to sleep
the reply… I can't
Just watch the power
and beauty in the potential
of disaster then, baby

Moon Children

I wonder if moon children know
How close they follow the tide of their mother
They are her favourite sights and sounds
Andromeda
The pipes, both small and large
Saturn with its ring
Even cold Mars with its red magik
Her gifts
Eternal

Scars

She wears her
Mother's scars
Wanting to die
Since she was 7 years old
Or fall asleep
Letting go the time passes by
Until the hurt
Sense of perceived
Abandoning
Dissipates
Thinking she could love them
Enough for herself
Themselves
And him
It was not
Not even close enough
And now her daughter wears
Her mother's scars

Break Ups

I cut her strawberries
in the hopes
Mohawk Medicine
can do something
for her bruised
heart

London

My little blue eyed iskwew
Freckles and blonde hair
The manifestation of my
Swedish blood
With Ceremonial Songs
Both Tradish and Florence
Ingrained in her
by 9 years old
Throws on Fleetwood Mac
'Mom, let's just cruise west'
My little highway girl

Daughters

I want my daughters
to have the attitude
of punk rock
and the grace
to carry it out
like a sunflower
reaching for the sun

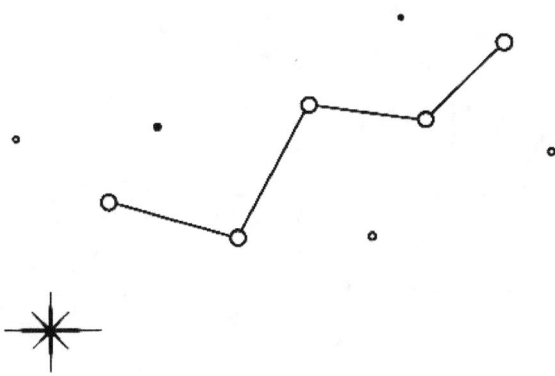

Lilacs

I know I typically thrive in fields of
raven roses, orchids
However
There is something so lovely
about pink and purple lilacs
who were caught in a cross wind
as I birthed my fourth blessing
at home surrounded by
women who loved him, me
Every year I am reminded
of my own strength
caught on the cross wind

Nature Vs Nurture

the way
he moves in and out
of violence
without shame
or a sense of
embarrassment
no apology
just begging to come
back home
after attempting to
light me on fire
reminds me
of his father

Pierce

so quiet

so sweet

I worry you get left behind

lost

in silence

working so hard to get

everyone to notice how

amazing you truly are

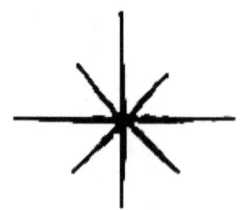

Webs and Fire Starters

Motherhood has been a series
Of cracks in my windshield
Webs of destruction
Letting fractured thoughts
                              Lights
                  Memories
Seep through
More blurred lines of tears
                Rage
       Fear
Uncertainty
Then of bliss and dreamy archetypes

I soak myself in hot water
Saturated in calendula, sea salt and oils
To repair matches striking my skin
Fists meeting my face and the ever present
I hate you
I wish you were dead
Vibrating through my ears

Phoenix

for a week I slathered
you in bear grease and
eucalyptus oil.
smudge heavy in the
air.
snuggles and naps.
I wish I could heal you
from all this anger
in the same way.
but, I cannot
and I am so sorry

Chael

when your baby looks like your father
you want to heal his hurts
to take away the memories
of a mother who abandoned
a father's hands who beat
kids who tormented and called names
by being a gentle, caring mother
one whose hands are steady

full of love
maybe it will heal all the hurts
of a father
of my childhood
he never meant to be

The Aftereffects of Domestic Violence

We move at the pace of love and oppositional defiance
disorder, now

Play

toes in mud
hands in rivers
Laughter in abundance
sunsets painted by angels
warm campfires
sleepy papoose
me, smiling
Healing

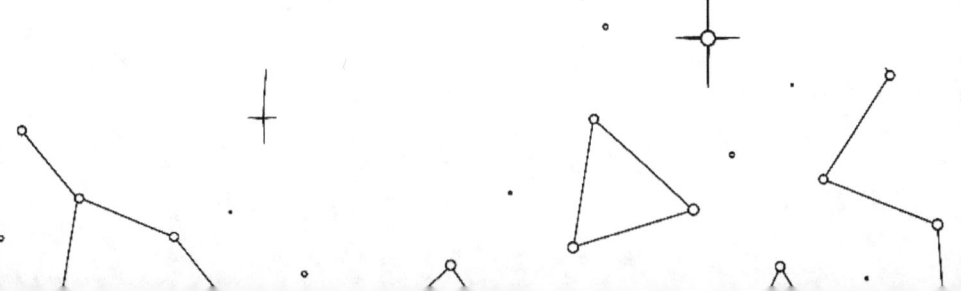

Who Are You?

I'm a deeply poetic, esoteric, spiritual
star-being that has a very difficult time
not returning to the skies. I stand on the
top of mountains to reach out and touch
the nearest nebula in order to stop myself
from leaving entirely. As a child I
believed I controlled the wind and would
test the loyalty of the gods and goddesses
by demanding weather changes as I lay in
the grass, interpreting the secret
messages in the clouds
convinced I was left behind by accident

When I am who I am, it's a homecoming for all

Crop tops
With
Old knit sweaters
Leggings
Thigh high socks
Knee high Docs
Tattoos
Rings
Necklaces
Earrings
Bed head hair
Kinda messy
Kinda makes
You want more

Homecoming

A homecoming of sorts

Candles

Incense

Card readings

Faeries

Sun

Moons

Embraced by the mystical

Feels so fucking good to be home

Chance

Putting my money
On that quiet one
Reading Warsan
The one who seeks
Solace in the mountains
The one who smells like
Sunlight and Sweetgrass

Paskwawimostos

I'm my name
The one
Close to Earth
Grazing
Who turns
To face the storm
Beside you
Steady
Strong
Even when
You're the one who
Summoned
These dark skies

Libra Suns

October tied up in lace and bound in leather
pretending to be a decent member of society

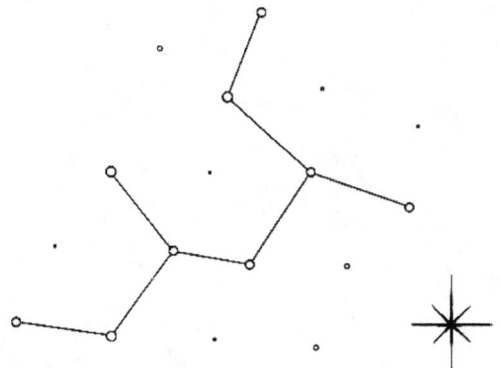

Fascinating

Watching me bend
                        b e n d
                                    b e n d
anticipating the crack
rather you
witness the collapse
into myself
the implosion
explosion
of my magik
nebulas
floating
as my star dust
settles
into my latest version
of strange and beautiful

I am my own galaxy

Moon Dust

I am
as ancient
as the moon dust
settled
on earth
forming bones
my words
warmth
run from this
earthly flesh
blood
but still, I remain true
to my star beings
cold
and everything in between
entirely beguiling

Energy Shift

It is easy to
Be intimidated
By me
You can see
All of my Degrees
Hanging on the wall
You witness me
Drumming
And singing
At Marches
You can read
My words
Published
In prose
journalism
My experiences
In podcasts
and
medical journals
I am vibrant
passionate
and I refuse
to be smaller
than what you want
me to be
making it easy to leave
and say
I am difficult

Collapse

the beauty is not
always in my
grace
the
way I
explode
falling into
myself
is also a
natural phenomena
you watch from afar

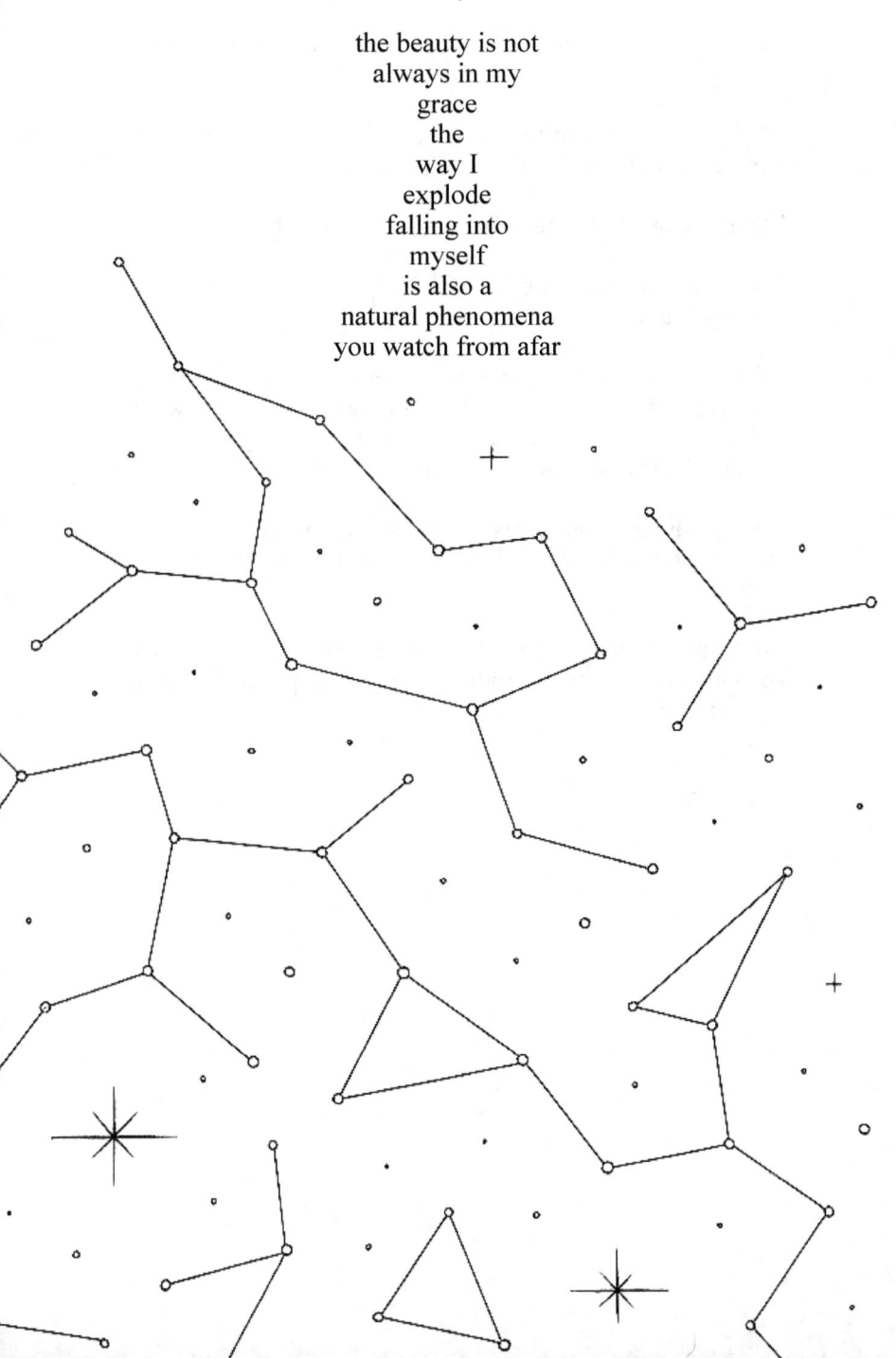

Love Letters to myself on my birthday

I love my slightly crooked teeth. I am not ever perfect. I am me.

My lips that kiss hurt tiny toes, speak soothing words to help hurt hearts and ooze honey into my lover's ears.

I love my laugh. It's full. Hearty. Recognizably mine.

My hands. Firm. Gentle. Tattooed. Open to giving and receiving healing.

Which, of course, brings me to my heart. Large, no stranger to being scarred, alas, it beats on. For another day, growing, relishing in the love it receives. From myself, my children, my family, my friends, the strangers in the streets.

My legs, long, strong, capable of leading marches, dancing, tobogganing, swimming, hiking and everything else in between.

My toes dig into the ground. A reminder to give thanks. To keep my connection as mother to others deep, nourished and replenished.

Loving The Mother of Storms

First you hear the winds
Howling In the fields
The city
Your ears
Bare skin
Exposed
Senses heightened
You witness the dark purple
Opaque clouds full of power
Her children, bold thunder
Demand to be heard
Never to be outdone
by their boisterous brothers
The sisters, touch down
Wreaking havoc, splitting trees
Causing wildfires
Soon to be directly overhead
Rolling over the dark greys
Gaining momentum
You cannot lie
How much you love the beauty in her destruction
Of everything that surrounds you
Your skin is not raised because you are wet
Chilled to the bone by the pouring rains
No
You are smiling
Excited
To be so loved by the Mother of Storms

Turns out it was me
who was all magikal and shit

The men
I
Thought
Were magik
All
Had me
In common

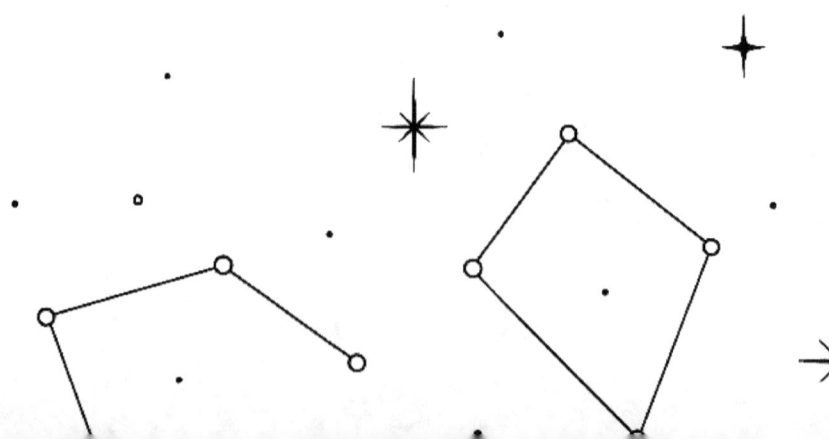

Smoked Salmon

Relationships: Fantasy, Dating, Sex and Break Ups

Metaphysical

I grew up atheist
Which comes as a surprise
My introduction to something
More than me was Ouija boards
Cold creatures pulling my leg under
Tarot cards read on top of the pentagram
Spirits looking for their lost child
Bright lights in the night skies
So
Don't be surprised when I don't want
To be lit like sage
Tumbling smoke
Held gently
And
I want to be Lillith
Powerful
On top
In control
Of my own
Pleasure
Where
You
Only
Wish
To
Be

Morning Skies

Silver tipped moon hugs their own curves.
just over top of Venus. Bold and true in
their natural state; love. The sky. Still.
Beautiful in her darkness. Calm,
watching, waiting. Their lover, the sun, is
chasing them. Sun comes for them at full
force. Pinks, oranges, red, fervent, eager,
impassioned. Tumbling over themselves.
A beautiful explosion. Sun, always
reaching as Moon smoothly disappears
into their midnight skies. Sun doesn't mind.

Love. Curses.

Is it a curse to be immediately loved by every man?
No. I do not believe love is a curse.

Demi sexual

I am not so concerned
About the way your flesh lays
As much
As the way
You carry a conversation
How your compassion
Fires off synapses
And the way you
Light up
When
You talk about
Someone you care for
This
Is
What I want

Basics

Adored and Devoured

Two basic needs

I'm going to require

From you

I refuse to accept anything less

Because I am so tired of

Constantly

Wanting more

Fantasy

You treat my romance

As fantasy

My reality

is

Ready for someone

To create fantasy

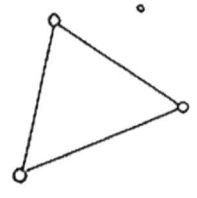

A Chance

I want you
More than pings
And hearts
I wanted a first
awkward date
concerts
hikes
late night baths
reading you poetry
I just wanted you
That's all

Healer

Gently, he took his thumb
Ran it up and over every knuckle
My palm opens
Pressed his lips in the center
Now, let's see what we can do
To heal you

Dark Moons. Dark Wolves.

walking back into the crowd
My Two Spirit Sister, looks at me
Low giggles, fixes my bangs
"you look a little ummm messy or should
I say mussed…lipstick is a bit smudged"
I smirk
My lip slightly curls
"we fucked in the back room"
"oh did you now?"
My eyebrow raises
"he can't stop looking at you, like, wolf
pacing outside a den, quiet, if you don't know
what you're looking at"
Flashes of hands pushing down clothing,
straps, skin on teeth, teeth on teeth, knees
bent, hips colliding, flesh on fire
Aware of time
Noticed absences
parting hastily
at separate times
re-entering at different doors
"he will always look at me like that
even when he's 80
with a softer belly
more greys in the hair
and beard
I will always be this night to him"
"mmm yes, yes you will be…
beguiling sex witch"

Dreams

He doesn't like the dreams
I have about him
It reduces
The
Conviction he
Has control at all
times

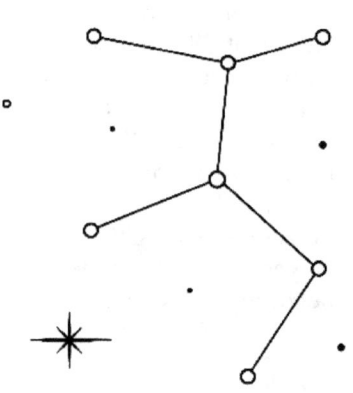

Flashes

The flashes remain
the same
arms wrap from behind
as he's hunched
over the piano
working out a melody
a murmured
How was your flight?
Kiss the back of his neck
Just holding this moment
Of him lost in creation
The notes slowly dwindle
Fingers clasp mine
Whispered
Come here
Hands lead me around to
standing in front of him
he presses his thumbs into my hips
the sound of me landing on the black and white keys
his low
fuck, I've missed you
as his dark needs
consume me

I Want To Lick His Brain

Fantasies
Existing in between
Keys, black and white
Moments
Of hesitation
Watching you get lost
Notes
Dissipate
Shift into
Lingering thoughts of your
Lips grazing along my neck

Mind F*ck

those beautiful
dark
minds
reaching
creating
painting
fantasies
quenching
infatuation
all the while
composing
fervor
for flesh to finally touch

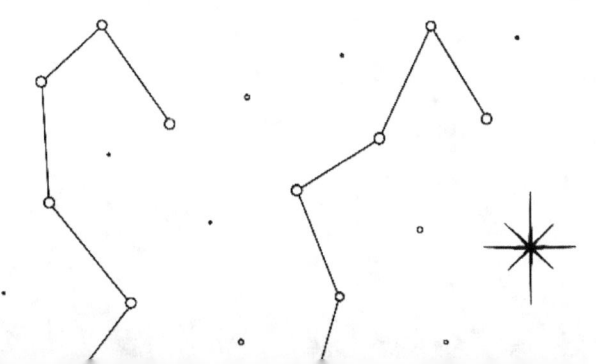

Shared Silence

The sun generous with
It's warmth
Grazing shoulders
Sitting on the dock
I picture your feet
Dipped in the lake
The ping of my message
As I'm sitting in the field
Of sage and roses
Both of us
Surrounded by dragonflies
Sharing silence
34000 km apart

Show Me Your Teeth, Wolf

Bringer of
Light
Why do you rest
So easily in your darkness?
Come here and I'll show you

Ethereal Rendezvous

Different nights
Full moons
Waxing moons
Same dream
My legs wrapped around
Your shoulders
Dark hair
Clenched between
My fingertips and palms
Sticky
Your skull rings pressed
Into my outer thighs

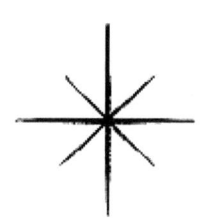

And, he's happy to be a part of my night

The piano
His voice
Rain falling
Pages turning
The sounds of my evening

Give me that gnarly man

Nice
Doesn't
Like poetry
About spanking
Gnarly
Replies back
That pink mark

What are we doing? When I think of you?

I think of
your
shoulders
my
long legs
your arms
wrapped under
me
grabbing your
dark hair
buried between my thighs

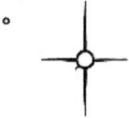

Learn her language

effort
into anything
is sexy
writing me
back
to say
you couldn't find it
in Cree
is a whole other level
of man

Captain

they're out there
the one who wants to
orchestrate your body
as though they're navigating their way
through the celestial seas

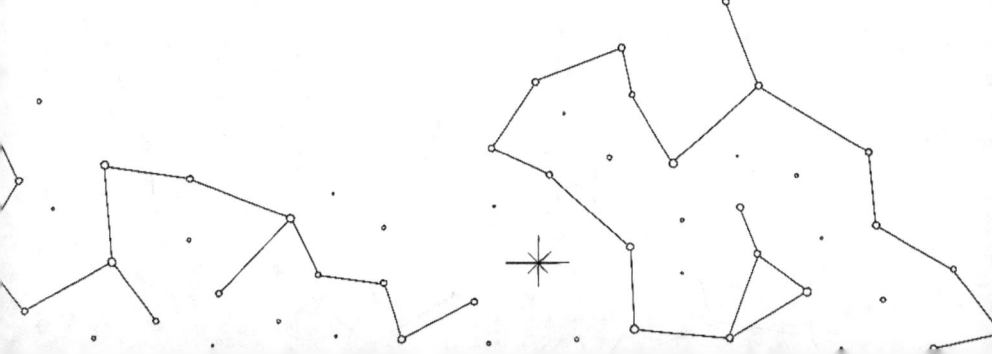

Make Men Feel

The lovely lay
draped in white sheets
a deep slumber
her thick dark hair
everywhere
likens to
spilled ink
a reminder
How she makes
mere mortal men
feel like
poets

Tinder & Tacos

In the time of
Tinder and Tacos
can I get some
love and loyalty?

Shut that shit down y'all

I will make you
Drive 2 hours to be shut down

Fuck boy needed a lesson

Date Night

meet me at the protest

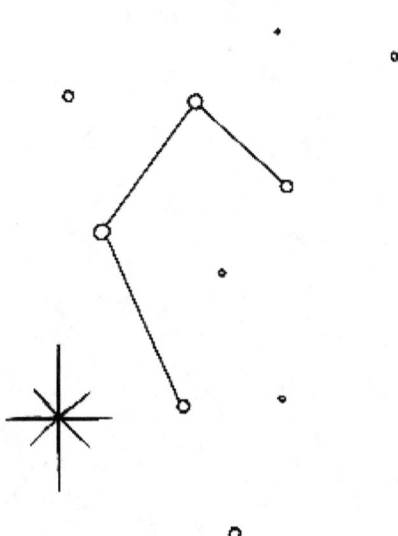

Dark Romance

Is not grand gestures
Draped in diamonds
It is quiet
Dark
2am musings
Of how much I miss
Reading
Whispering
Murmuring
Prose into their ears
Bathtubs
Hot water with oils
Flower petals
Submerged in intimacy
As I recite
My lust
My nails
Digging down
Their sides

Heat

eyes meet
striking of the
match
laughter
kindling
catches fire
fingertips
graze
crackling
of
logs
lips meet
renewed
heat

A Lover's Gaze

Don't break it now

Here

In front of everybody

I'm quietly

Undressing your

Soul

Here

In front of everybody

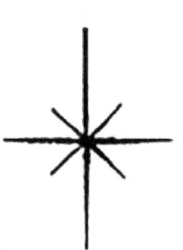

Gravitational Pull

Did you feel it too?

My warmth pulling you in

                        Under

My gravitational pull

Knows no bounds

Just like the Moon

I make the tides yearn

Constantly reaching and retreating

Come Over?

I miss lust
Tension
Spilling over
Fingertips
Patiently
Gripping
My
Hips
Your
Teeth
Sink
Into
My
Bottom
Lip

Nakedness is not a place of shame.
It's a natural state of love.

Accessibility
To my nudity
Is
Not the same
As my
Sexuality

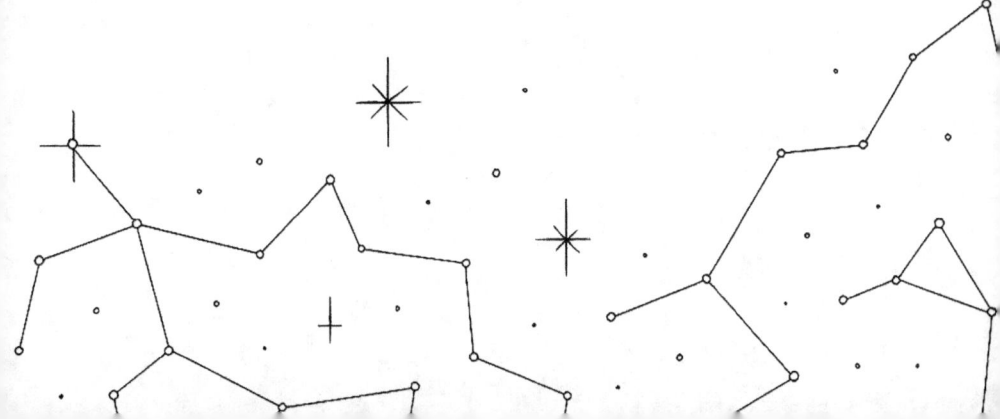

First, foreplay

There are all
The firsts
Clutching
Sheets
Fists
Full
Of
Hair
Nipples
Twisted
Distinctly
In between teeth

Ache

make their back arch

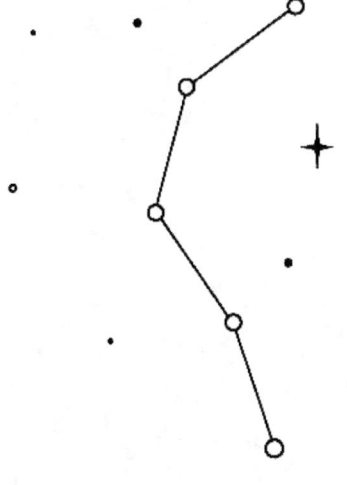

Partner Sex

In every shade of
Crimson
I want to burn
Cheeks flush
Sweat trickling
Down
My neck
Soft jaw
Deep moans

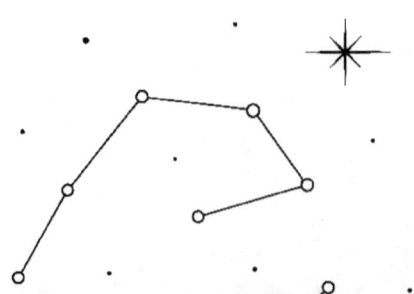
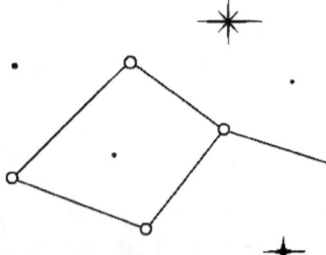

Good Morning

      I adore
       crave
       want
      idolize
       love
      relish
      yearn
      covet
     desire
    hunger
      pine
    savour
appreciate
  enjoy
         morning sex

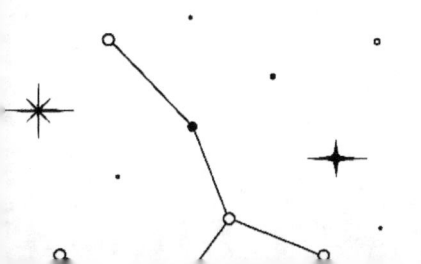

Miyo-kisikaw

I roll over
And feel the warmth
Of where your
Body once laid
Your scent
Still lingers
On the pillow
My skin
The
Silence
Of your
Absence
Broken
By a digital bleep
My screen lights up
…..good morning
What do you take in your tea?....

Witchy Women

These Witchy women

with Raven hair

Sunlit hair

Scarlet hair

Messy and unbound

Have particular needs

Candles

Binding leather

Deep red lips

Under the protection of the moon light

Witnessed at every phase

To feel their love unleashed

While tied

Is a ceremony

Few are fortunate to receive an invite for

Bind. Tie. Blind Fold. You Lead.
I Follow. I Submit

I don't want
To
Always
Be
In
Control

Bind Your Next Adventure

wrists to ankles

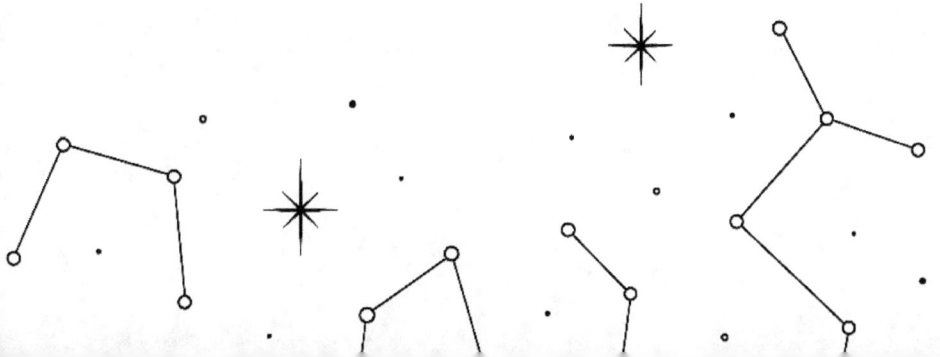

Suit Wearers

while I'm certain
that tie
(fingers fumble over knot)
took time
I'm more certain
(loosens tie)
I want you
(slides tie down)
to take the time
to
tie me up
(places hands out)

Real Tradish

Braids
And
Binds

Pull my hair in that sacred way

Breathless

I want his gentle hands
reaching

      sliding

            holding
       my hand

as much

as I want his rough hands
reaching

      sliding

            holding
       my throat

X Marks the Spot

all I want is to be
reminded of my
feminine
side
by
being
devoured
feasted upon
by the lone wolf

Worship

You worship at her feet

You worship her feet

You worship her

Worship her

Worship

Her

Queen of Desire

Your long legs
white toenails
Another one
Please
With the leopard print
heel
dangling
from behind
Over the shoulder
I want to see your
Plump, perfect, round
Ass
Pouty mouthed
Boss bitch face
Not come kiss me
I do not have time or lust for
Generic
Trout pout/blonde/brunette/redhead
I crave
The Queen of Desire

More

drenched in carnal lust
her eyes demand
more

you, as always
willingly oblige

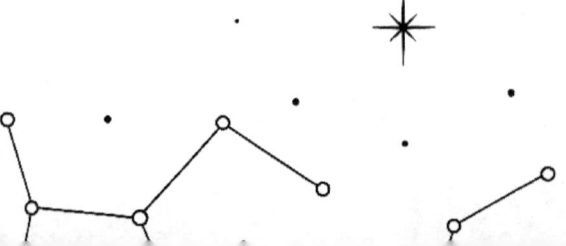
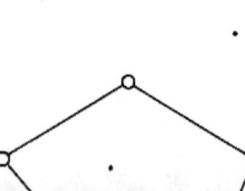

Statue

that time you were on my couch
the moonlight streaming in
the couch looks like the jet-black sky
it's actually navy blue
an ideal background
for your baby blues
and you
you looked like a living statue
sitting in the corner
gleaming
head back, panting
broad shoulders
thick thighed
resting, for another thousand years.

Dark Needs

The ways
I pressed back
Into your kiss
Heavy panting
Deep moans
Perpetual wetness
Tongues linger
Showing you
How much
I relish in your
Darker needs
Will always haunt you

Versions of Bliss

bite
my teeth
suck
my tongue
my toes
fuck
me senseless
directionless
timeless
complete
sense
of
bliss

Honey

love cascaded
thick as honey
from her lips
    to your tongue
from her hips
    to your tongue

Women as Mountains

Mountains
Are women
Laying naked
On their back
On their side
Deep green bushes
Wet blue lakes
White nipple peaks
Dark caves
Sacred
Exploration

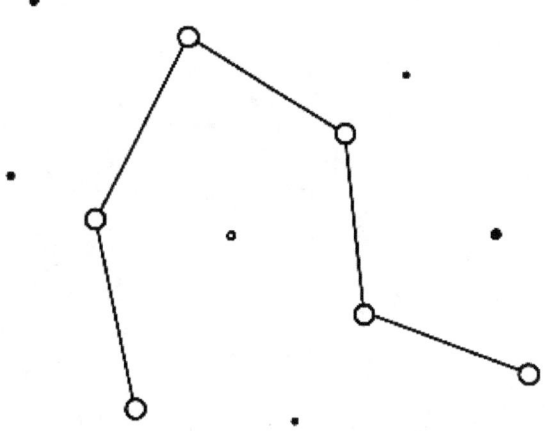

Awoken

she kissed her back
tracing her
fingertip
from shoulder
tip
to
shoulder tip
she could hear the
slight shift in her
breath
from gentle
rhythmic
to shallow
in anticipation
where those
lips
and fingertips
would next explore

Patterns

Still not sure
If
It's the way
The stockings
Pattern
Hugged my hips

The way you
Gripped my hips

Or

The way
You ripped
The material
To get in between
My hips

That you
Think about most

Indulge

Mystic
Mythic
Psychic
women are where I indulge

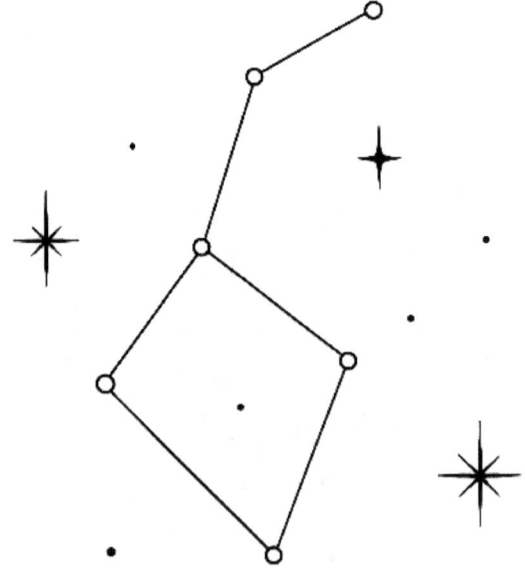

Word Me

I want to be drenched
in poetry
lavished
in
your
attention

Where Dark Needs Meet Light Tendencies

I would be lying
if I said I didn't
want dark romance
full of crescent moons
lace, leather, and ties
but
I also want grand
adventures
of meet me at
the airport
pack up the trailer
live music
a balance of
everything
I want

Relationships

Not
One who
Wants
To settle
Down
With you
Rather
One who
Wants
To run
Your
Wild with
You

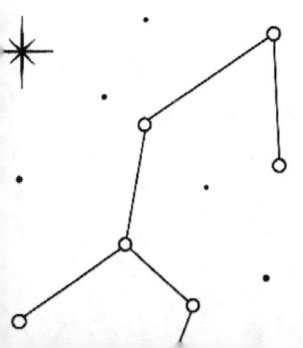
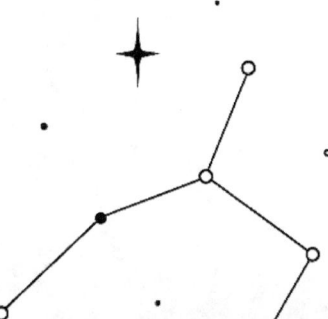
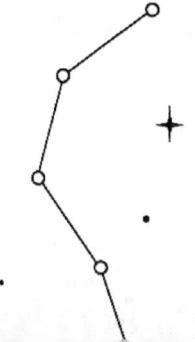

Who do I Love?

You. Always you.
Every single magikal atom, you

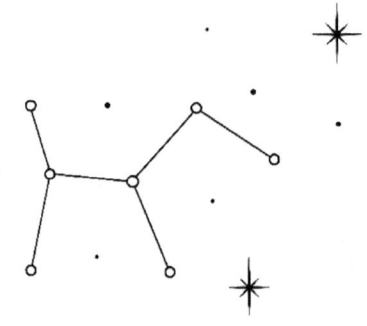

I Don't Want Anything Else

Bring me
Peace
And
Pleasure

Tender hearted

Only take on
Lovers
Whose touch
Is an extension
Of their words

Release the lonesome to the fire
in the form of tobacco
and let yourself be tender

The warmth
Of a fire
Low
Crackling
As I snuggle
Deeper
Into the heavy
Fur
Of that wolf
Fiercest
Protector
As I lay
In vulnerability

Promises

whispers
between
lips and ears

hair
wrapped around
knuckles

pinky fingers
intertwined
under stars

Wrap Me in Poetry

Let your tender words
Roll off your lips
Flow into my ears
As they find their way into my bloodstream
Land in my heart
Fingertips roll over keys
Melody
Chorus
Murmurs
Intimacy lingers in the air

Bedside

Why do you lay on your side of the bed?
When it is only you
There is no me/you
What are you scared of?
Rolling over ghosts of lovers
Relationships passed
Feeling your heart
Race
Release
Break
From the memories laced
Into sheets
Scents
Between fibres
Once clenched
In between fingertips
Don't give them that space
It is your bed after all
And
You're still here
In this bed
Your bed

Full Moons. Spring Fever

on these dark nights
I want to feel the
rush of lust
in the form
of fingertips
reaching
sliding
your sultry mouth
feeds on my shoulder
teeth, bared
not holding back
consume
me
whole

Radio Silence

I miss the way you call me gorgeous
With my
Strength and grace

Less is not More

Less common sense
Less compassion
Less kindness
Less passion
Less knowledge
Less awareness
Less lust
Less humour
Less listening
Less of everything I actually wanted
Because at least he looked in my direction

Trickster

He wasn't a bad spirit, after all.
But still a trickster.
Shape shifting his way into her bed.
Her head.

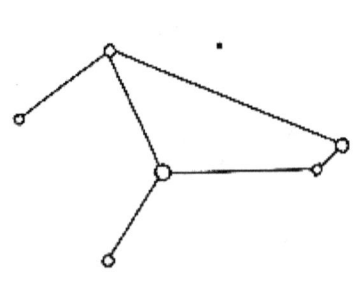

Tinder

He will go out feasting
Trying to rid the
Memory
Taste
Of
Me

Why

Loving you is effortless
Why is this complicated?

Puzzle Piece

When you told her
You are my missing puzzle piece
Where sky meets ground
My horizon
My Moon
My Star
What happens when she walks away
Back to the supernova she was conceived in that
Has the most beautiful moonsets
She's still whole
Sweet, lovely, maddeningly gorgeous
What happens to you, though?
You look for her in sunsets, sunrises, poetry
Failing
Miserable
Right back where she found you

Release

Slowly
I strip your scent
From
My skin
Sex
From my sheets

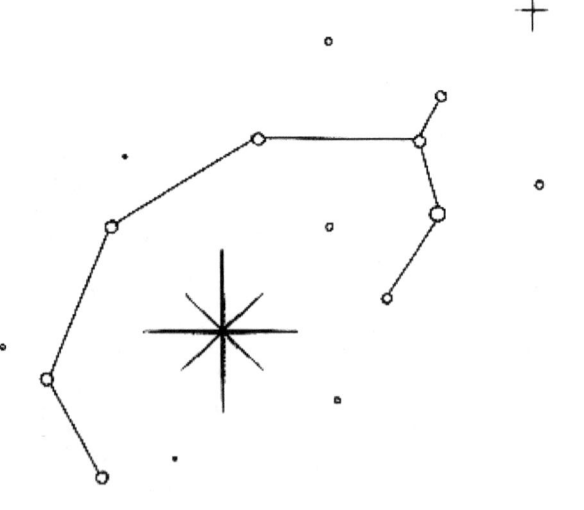

In My Head

....Red Wine
....Whiskey

Landed me in his bed
Because you're in my head

Midnight Whiskey

I don't drink whiskey
Anymore

The midnight thoughts
Of you though

Those linger on my
Tongue

Sickly
Sweet mix of
Regret and longing

Secrets

I could hold all your secrets for you
Put them in a can
Soothe all the hurts
Love you
Enough
So you could begin to heal

However……………..

I will not be your secret

Chose

I chose me.

One of us had to.

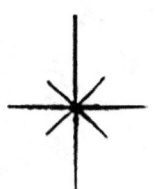

Intentions

You know
The Ancestors
Sky Beings
Star Beings
Watch over me

What
Exactly
Were
Your
Intentions

Act Right

       I laid my
        Heart
        Fears
       Tobacco
        Down
        For You

You acted as though you've never seen ceremony before

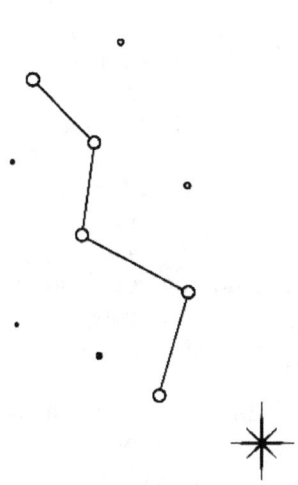

The After Math of You

rooting back
into myself
I crawl under
my own ribs
caress my heart
whisper
hold her
remind her to
expand until
she feels the safety
of my own ribs
who hold her up
and in

As
the sorrow
flows from my eyes
the taste of my
own heartbreak

rolls off my
lips
onto my mat

the act of self
love
is slowly
removing you from my
marrow
and allowing
myself to heal
In ways I know how
move
nourish
love

One Day

One day I won't be here

In pieces strewn

Across the floor

Scrambling to pick them up

Large pieces

Small pieces that are only visible by the glint they make in

the sunlight space

Gently holding them in my palm

Bloodied, tired fingers

Always fixing, always repairing

Wiping away tears

Leaving blood smears

For all those years

I'm Safe

you're safe I'm here
you're safe 'm here
you're safe m here
you're safe   here
you're safe   ere
you're safe   re
you're safe   e
    you're safe
    you're safe

Scar Upon Scar

I peeled back my flesh
broke my own bone
removed the marrow that
held onto you

and began again

Sacred Space

Pick up a stick
Draw a circle
In the sand
Me
In the center

See that circle
That space
Is sacred

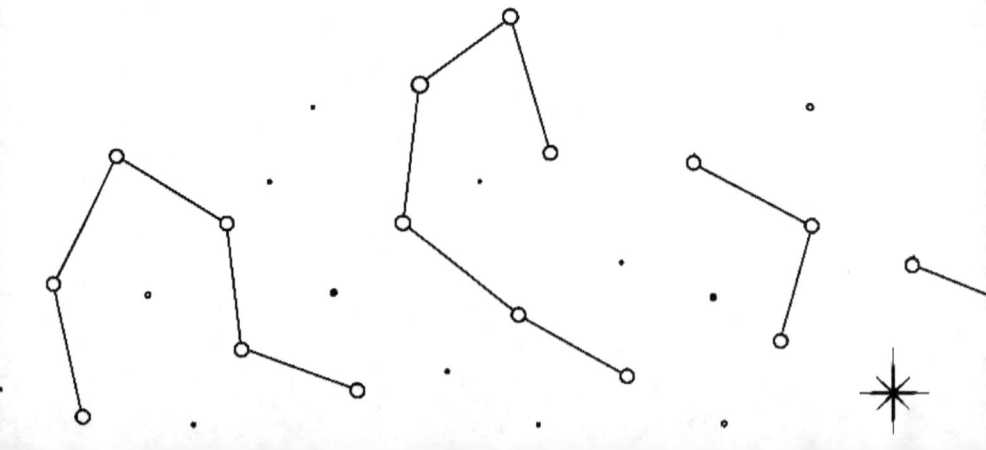

Crescent Moon & Venus

As the waning moon leans in to kiss the elusive Venus. Shy. Unassuming. Doesn't want the whole galaxy to see the intimate moment. Moon whispers to Venus, oh, but who cares. I want everyone to see. Every Nebula, every Star, every Planet, every other Moon, to know I'm only ever here for you. Venus, nervous, accepts the gesture. And for two nights, the once under cover lovers shine to show galaxies what it means to kiss.

Celebrate. Spring Fever. Spring Showers.

Some lovers'
Bodies feel so much like home
That the sweat
That pours off their
Brow onto your back
Is celebrated
Like the first rain
In spring

Celestial Dancer

Gently, he
Glides into
Venus
Shifting sights
Onto Milky Way
Lapping her up
Across her
Entire body
Seduces….. slowly
Orange, Pink and Purple
Nebulae
Until only one
multi-coloured
dust cloud remains
Now near
Approaching Moon
The esoteric Empyrean Queen

Time Disappears

Sense of time disappears
Like Eros into the spheres
of their lover
Eyes
…Open…
….Close.…
…Light…
..Dark..
Twilight
Sunset
Sunrise

….

A Million Years Ago

in
above
out
below
the
energy
leads
you astray
of within
now
without

Ascend in the Descension

thoughts descend
ego is sacred
ascends body
ideas crash,
egos smash.
bodies collide
mind's eye hides

Taken Care Of

I want
Soft
To be
Land
Embraced
Cause I know all
Too well how to survive
Hard

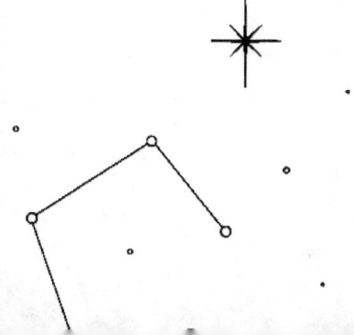
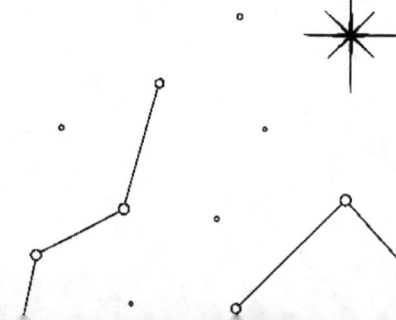

Spring Days

Delicate traipsing

Fresh rained on grass

Green. Softened earth. Smell of dirt.

Cozy.

Old books. Old blankets.

heavy with memory and goose feathers.

Tea steeping. Coffee brewing.

Your warmth. Your smell.

The comfort of it all.

Rainy Days

come back to bed
warm my soul

Winter

winter was made for
making love
warm beds
sipping
tea
coffee
eating chocolate
and
naps

Rise

You rise

I crawl

On top

My warmth

Welcomes you

Slowly

Embraces you

Whole

sun

Cascading in
Lingers on my
Neck....
Collar bone....
Close my eyes
Tilt my head backwards
Bask in his warmth
Gently grazing
My cheekbone....
Tip of my nose....
Top lip....
Embraced by my sun

warmth

surely you miss the
warmth of
me
wrapped
around you

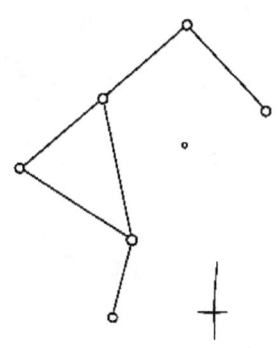

Snowed In

small cabin in the woods
Fire belly stove
kettle on
tea
books
poetry
scripts
snowed in
one warm bed

Nothing Out of The Ordinary

I had this dream

Nothing out of the ordinary

I was in a hot bath

Dimly lit

Oils

Reading poetry

Nothing out of the ordinary

I felt you under me

You were reading

I turned my head closer into your chest

Looked up at you

And I felt it

Calm

Serene

Warmth

You kissed my forehead

And we both returned back to reading

Nothing out of the ordinary

Exhale

I'd wake up to you
Laying on your stomach
Half covered in sheets
Gently tracing my chin
Following my jawline upwards
Softly thumbing my earlobe
Up and over the tops of my ears
Slowly sweeping my cheekbone

I'd look at you through half open eyes
Not wondering what you were doing

Because your eyes
Show the disbelief
Of me here in your bed
Still
After all these years
Of what ifs, bad timing, could haves
She's here
And very much real

No more restless nights
4am wake ups
Lonely

The quiet
Is broken
By your exhaled
"I love you"

Giver

Don't ever regret the way you love
Freely
with passion
without shame
A giver of love
Is a superpower
in this too often
Emotion hoarding
World

Sex is Ceremony

Sex is Ceremony
Sex is powerful
Sex is healing
Sex is fun
Sex is love
Sex is intimate
Sex is giving
Sex is receiving
Sex is sacred
Sex is Ceremony

Sweet Treats

The Ceremony that holds me
through it all

Lodge and Life Teaching

Chop wood
Haul water

Writing Process

burn your medicines
let your truth spill

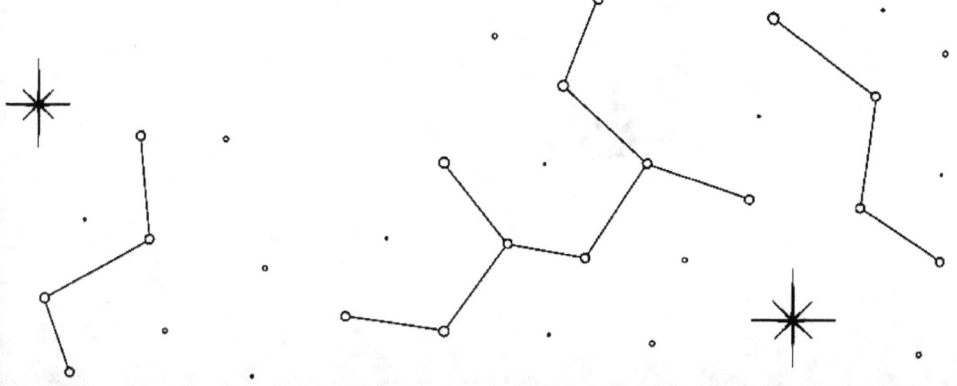

Surrender

there is no door
to call open
there is no breaking
a fast
there is no call
to support and switch
there is, you
baby
and the
ceremony
that is
birth

Birth Worker

The need for balance
at the point
where colours blend
together.
The Connector.
The Healer.
In a solitary realm
surrounded by
tremendous purpose.
And now,
sisterhood.

Birth Worker Wisdom

those Thunderbeings
love to coax
babies
Earth side
don't they

October

give me hot baths
scented with lavender
oils and petals
the air thick with
sage, cedar, sweetgrass
and
Nina Simone
making the candlelight
dance
as my body and soul
float in peace
my mind finally
at ease

Healing Waters

Salts

Oils

Splashes on the rocks

Sweat

Salt in the eyes

Bear oils

Music

Drums

Songs

Connecting to my relations

Inner divinity

Inner light

Edge of Discomfort

as you find the
edge of discomfort
explore
breathe
release
and then
lean into it
just a little bit more
let it shift
into a place
of
comfort

Mama Two Shoes

still
the nights
I cry for you
Wishing for your
Lap to lay my head on
Listen to you sing
Drums and rattles
Steam swirling
Around us
Still

Year 2

This morning, as we lit sage, cedar, and sweetgrass
all picked, braided and ground by my hand
we gave our prayers to you
you, as always, showed us
how warm, beautiful and bold your love truly is

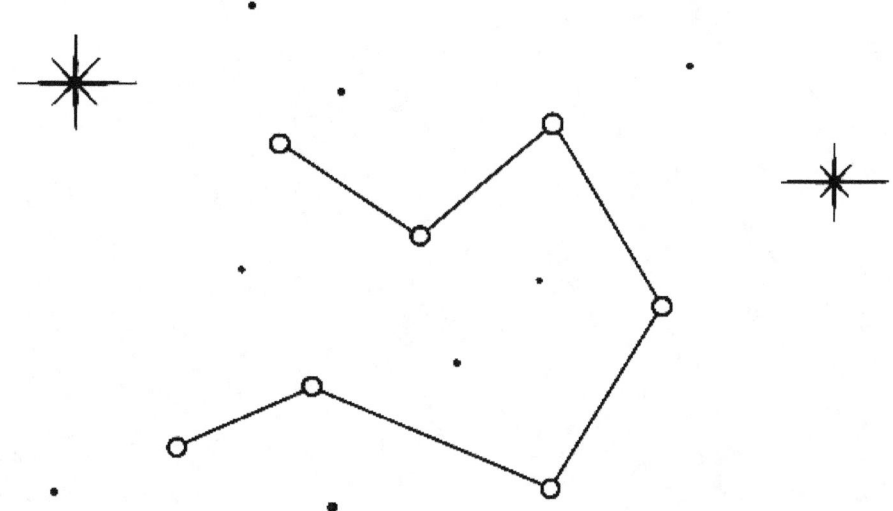

Exploring Red Willow

Let's move unread
Smooth red
Limbs
Layers
It's not just the
Medicine in the center
We
Seek every sensation
It's every piece
Part
That makes it so sacred

Grandfather Stones

My soul is safe
tenderly cared for
By the grandfather stones
Whose spirits I lie on my chest
To keep me from ascending away
Into the night sky

Grandmother Moon

she greets me
in her light
gives the space
to rest
release
everything
and remind me
I am whole
in every
phase

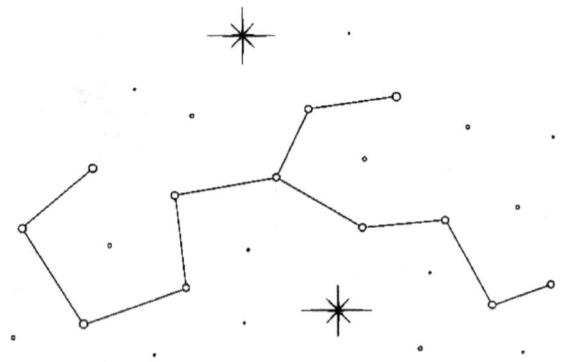

Original Mother

remember the first
time you laid
in the green grass
the wind
was no longer
moving the small blades
rather the whole
terrain underneath
you was heaving
shifting
breathing
gently rolling your tiny fingertips
through her short hair
as you thanked
the first mother

Webs

Grandmother spider
I wish I had never-ending
Creativity
Your endless supply of
Silky string
Is jealousy provoking
I watch you without effort
Nimbly
Lay out a pattern that's never
To be duplicated
Your delicate, intricate, sinewy web
Is a force of nature
And if done by sunrise
A place to catch the morning dew
A shimmering sight to behold
I wish to only create something
Similar
To catch
The occasional haiku

Look, even when we aren't asking for medicine, we receive them

I had a dream that I was eating soup infused with sweet grass, a whole braid. I was explaining, softly, to a little brother, who was eating a delicate piece of meat, why there were medicines in my soup. He scooped out the best piece of meat, all without asking or looking for it.

Reciprocity

Bring me the trees.
Their roots underfoot, stronger than the
winds sent from the Ocean, providing
strength for over 800 years.
Upon my death
Let my body rot in the trees; so that my
body may return to the mother,
nourishing the dirt, my soul released to
dance back to the ancestors.
The natural balance of life and death
Continues

Acknowledgements

It took me six years of writing, curating, editing, and sourcing, for this collection to come earth side. Hand to heart to my mom for always encouraging me to follow my dreams. To my kiddos for validating their weird, witchy mom by buying my poetry and teacups, and allowing me to write about them. Kinananskomitin Barb, my biggest cheerleader and heart center. To Beric, who let me write him odes for his birthday—something I had never done before. To Alyjah for introducing me to everyone as a midwife that writes poetry and is a Two Spirit storyteller. To Dan for being the best promo guy I never did hire. The Wolf for saying yes to late night requests of my version of romance. To all my queer and Two Spirit kin, you are everything good that life has to offer. Thank you, Kait, for editing. Thank you to Alexis at Wild Skies Press for bringing this long-time dream to print. And, of course, Sharron; with whom I shared my dreams of writing poetry and the excitement of embarking on this new adventure as she was about to set out on hers, back to the stars.

Alycia Two Bears

Bio

Alycia Two Bears, a mixed-blood iskwew from Mistawasis Nêhiyawak First Nation, calls Mohkinstsis home. Alycia holds degrees in General Studies and Education from the University of Calgary. She combines her expertise as a certified yoga instructor with Traditional 2 Spirit Métis-Cree teachings in her Land-Based Yoga practice, fostering a connection between body, breath, and ceremony.

A mother of five, she is a passionate advocate for birth sovereignty. Alycia practices Birthing as Ceremony and aspires to become a midwife. She supports pregnant and birthing bodies, working to ensure accessible, dignified care. Through grassroots initiatives and collaboration, she co-created the Moon Time Bag Initiative. To end period poverty, Alycia redistributes donated menstrual health products to houseless and housed kin.

An award-winning poet and writer, Alycia has contributed to publications such as Red Rising Magazine, MBC Magazine and New Tribe Magazine. Her work often centers on decolonization, mental health, and Two Spirit advocacy. Recognized for her community impact, she received The Advocate for Equality Award from the Calgary Single Mother's Society and USAY Change Makers award. Alycia's passions include decolonizing systems, uplifting her community, and nurturing her family's connection to nêhiyawân language and culture.

Instagram: @your.moon.woman

Headshot: Studio Lumen

Other Books from Wild Skies Press

www.WildSkiesPress.com

www.ingramcontent.com/pod-product-compliance
Lightning Source LLC
Chambersburg PA
CBHW070425010526
44118CB00014B/1901